THE BUTTERFLY EFFECT

THE BUTTERFLY EFFECT

Victoria Richardson

VR

V Rich Publishing Company

"For my mother, who
taught me the love of
stories, and my father, who
lived them."

"Butterflies recognize the beauty in transformation."

Table of Contents

The
Love

My life changed the day I met you....

I touched your face, I kissed your lips, I clutched
your hands, I took naps with you, I washed your
hair, I cried my eyes out, I did everything to show
love and those effects changed everything....

and now that your gone it's like you took what
you needed from me.... and left me alone.
-The Butterfly Effect

No more fake love for you to
give.
No more mistakes for you to
forgive.
The memories are all gone.
My life is back to the way it
should be.
I can finally start back to loving
me.
The fake love is being used on
another
I hope they can see your true
colors.

-Fake Love

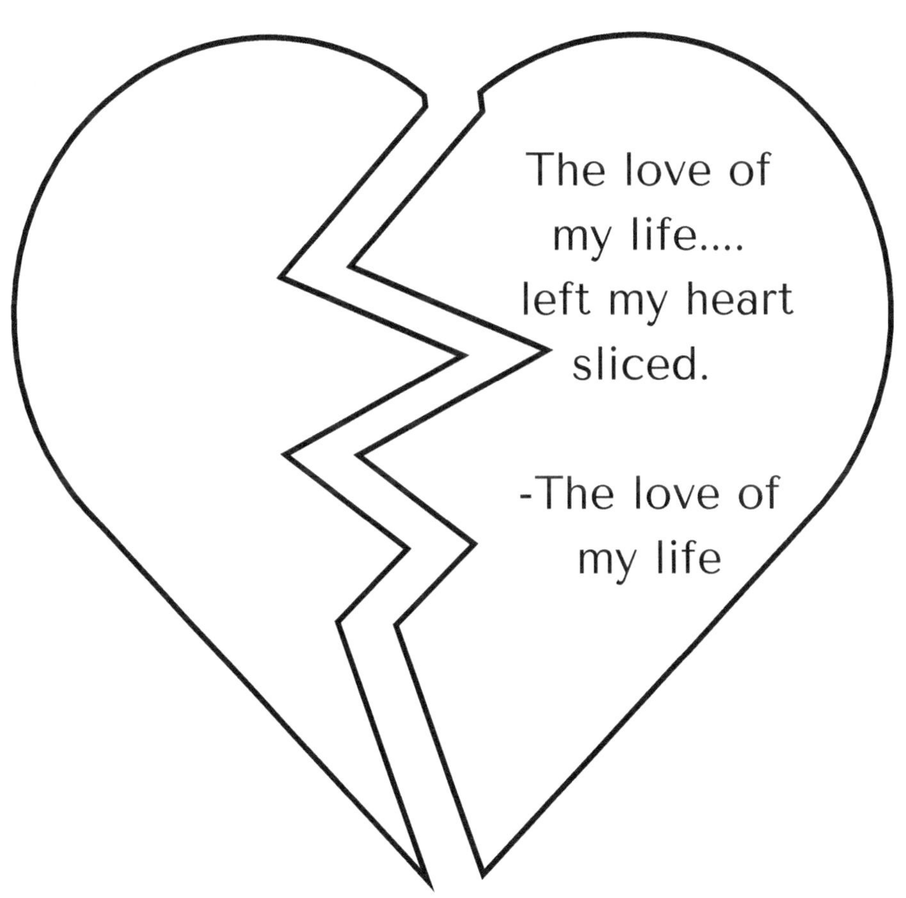

The love of
my life....
left my heart
sliced.

-The love of
my life

The love is gone...
So I can move on.

Popcorn love, a fleeting treat, Sweet and salty, oh so neat. A kernel's pop, a moment's bliss, In love's embrace, we find our kiss.

Each bite a crunch, each kiss a spark, In popcorn love, we leave our mark. With laughter shared and hands entwined, Our love pops loud, a joyful find.

But like popcorn kernels, we may stray, In different directions, we may sway. Yet when we're together, we ignite anew, In popcorn love, forever true.

So let's savor each moment, each savory bite, In popcorn love, our hearts take flight. For in the simplicity of kernels popped, We find the essence of love, never stopped.

"Less is more" encourages us to focus on quality rather than quantity — investing our time and energy into pursuits that align with our values and passions, rather than spreading ourselves thin across a multitude of endeavors. By decluttering our lives — both physically and mentally — we free ourselves from the burden of excess, allowing room for creativity, inspiration, and inner peace to flourish.

Every now
and
than I have to
remind
myself to
breathe.

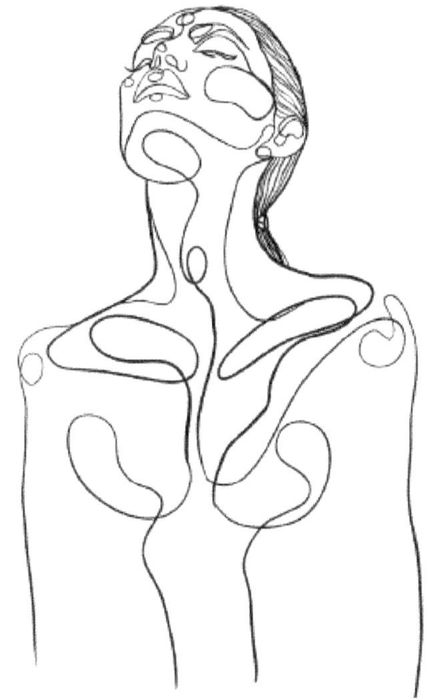

You
interrupted
my peace,
just to break
my heart...

Love yourself.
Be good to
yourself.
Embrace change.
give the love you
never had to

yourself.

It's difficult to find love again after dating a conceited individual. You become accustomed to their absurd notion of love's highs and lows and eventually stop trusting people.

The Loss

I begged you to stay with tears in my eyes, but you couldn't wait to leave....

I felt like
someone had
taken me off of
a tremendously
strong
prescription
medicine the day
you abandoned
me.

1. "Deleting a narcissist from your life is not an act of cruelty, but an act of self-preservation and self-love."
2. "Removing a narcissist from your life is not about losing them, but about finding yourself again."
3. "Cutting ties with a narcissist is not a sign of weakness, but a testament to your strength and resilience."
4. "Letting go of a narcissist is reclaiming your power and freedom from their manipulation."
5. "Deleting a narcissist from your life is like deleting toxicity from your soul, paving the way for healing and growth."

This is heavy.
This is pain.
But in your absence, my days
are never full of rain.
-The End of Stormy Weather

The day I lost
you was the
day I
discovered
who I was...

The day I buried you was a day of
turmoil...
I hated myself for using good soil.
You never made me feel whole.
I needed you to stop haunting my
soul.
I needed to bury you in my back
yard
I needed to let myself know that
leaving you alone wasn't hard.

-Buried

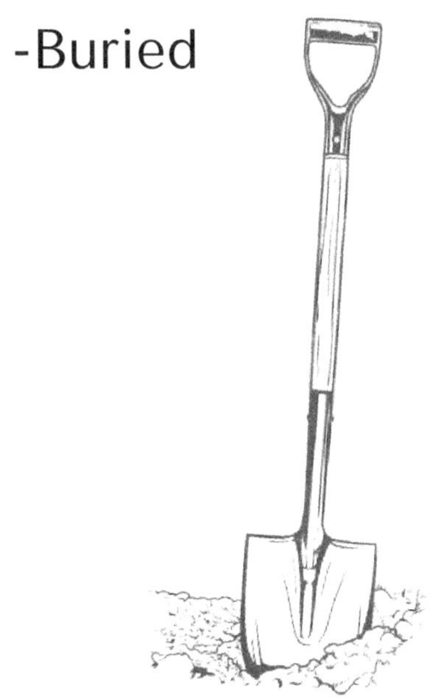

Waiting for the right words to end this war.

Maybe this argument won't leave a hole in my door.

We fight...

All night.

You tell me everything will be alright.

You hold me tight.

We makeup.

We breakup.

All the words I said was unheard...

They are nothing but wasted words.

-Wasted words

I'm not your punching bag.

"Sometimes the bravest thing you can do is let go of the one who is holding you back, even if it means stepping into the unknown alone."

I felt it in my soul to let you go
be a man on your own....
I learned that holding on to
you....made me feel alone.
-Alone

The Passion

The art of healing.
It demands time.
It requires work.
It demands affection.

- The Art of healing

You needed me.
I was your oxygen.
You was my flame.
We were opposites....
But we needed each other to remain.

-Needed Me

Detours are necessary

They suggested veering off course. Considering how chaotic my life already was, I questioned why I would need to take a detour. I felt abandoned fast. I was tired from having to decide which way to travel because the first option, while easy to follow, was very dangerous. However, the distraction was terrifying, full of twists and turns, and there were a lot of lessons to be discovered. It was a long detour, but one that was needed.

Healing is never easy.
Breathing becomes wheezy.
You survived the rain.
But pain still remains.

-Healing Hurts

I don't believe in soul mates,
I barely have a soul.

In her heart, a kingdom's grace, A Queen's love for her King, embrace. Through trials and triumphs, hand in hand, Their love, a bond no one could withstand.

In the art of letting go, there's grace,
A gentle release, a newfound space.
Like autumn leaves, we surrender
the old, Embracing the beauty in
letting unfold.
Through whispered sighs and quiet
tears, We bid farewell to our doubts
and fears. For in the freedom of
release, we find, A lightness of
heart, a peace of mind.

Healing feels like....

Healing feels like....sleeping in late.
Going on spontaneous dates.
Ignoring unnecessary emails and phone calls.
Learning to let go and fall.

Healing feels like.... kissing under a starry sky.
Shooting shots at that handsome guy.
Road trips to uncharted places.
Meeting new and familiar faces.

Healing feels like.... finding yourself on a beach.
Giving yourself freedom of speech.
Finding happiness in little things.
Loving what life brings....

At last I feel alive!
I'm no longer numb inside
The pain of heartache no longer lingers.
The soul ties have slipped out of my
fingers.

-At Last

Pain On Paper

Her pain is on paper.
She is hurting, so who will save her?
No time for her to be weak.
She opens her mouth and tries to
speak.
Her pain is on paper.
The love she had betrayed her.

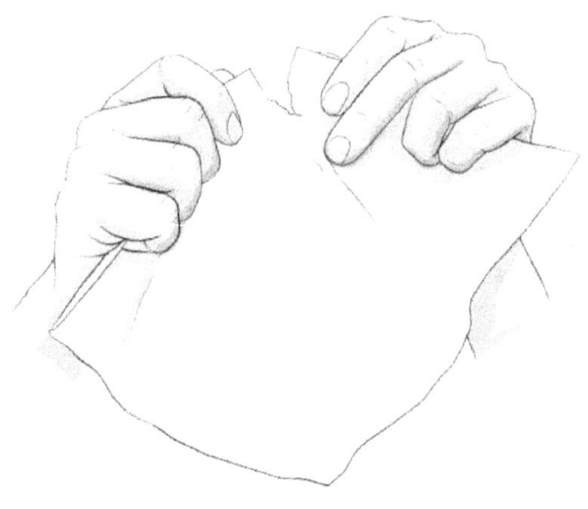

The Beauty

Feeling like "Sleeping Beauty" during a breakup can be a metaphorical journey. Just as Sleeping Beauty was in a deep slumber until awakened by true love's kiss, someone going through a breakup might feel emotionally dormant, waiting for a spark to revive their sense of self-worth and happiness. Initially, it might feel like being in a state of hibernation, withdrawn from the world and cocooned in sadness.

However, like the fairy tale, there's a potential for transformation and awakening.

Much like Sleeping Beauty's eventual awakening, healing from a breakup involves time, self-care, and sometimes the support of loved ones. It's about rediscovering one's inner strength and beauty, despite the pain.

Paper planes, in graceful flight,
Paint the sky with pure delight.
In their arcs, I see a tale, Of
wonder,joy, and love's travail.
With every fold, a journey starts,
A testament to creative hearts.
In their beauty, I find awe,
In paper planes, I see love's law.

In heartbreak's depth, a beauty lies, A
bittersweet melody, a mournful sigh.
Through shattered dreams, new paths
unfurl, In tears shed, the soul's true
pearls.
From endings sprung, beginnings take
flight, In the darkness, we find our
inner light. For in the ache of a love
now lost, We learn to cherish what it
truly cost.
So let the pain carve valleys deep, For
in its wake, new treasures we'll keep. In
heartbreak's embrace, we find our art,
A testament to the resilience of the
human heart.

In mirrors gazed, his ego thrives, A master
of deceit, with honeyed lies.
With charm so potent, yet cold as ice,
He weaves his web, a dangerous device.
His love, a poison, sweet and cruel,
Leaving hearts broken, a painful fuel.
A narcissist, with eyes that gleam,
His love a mirage, a fleeting dream.
He moves on swiftly, to new supply,
Leaving behind tears, a silent cry.
In his wake, shattered hearts remain,
Victims of his charm, victims of his game.
But though he seeks new faces fair,
His reflection haunts him, always there.
For in the end, he's trapped alone,
A prisoner of his own ego's throne.

In the aftermath of a stormy departure,
I stand, a solitary figure, amidst the
wreckage Of shattered dreams and
fractured promises.
Once entangled in the web of your
deceit, I now emerge, a phoenix from
the ashes, Reclaiming my essence, my
truth, my worth.
Your narcissistic grip, once suffocating,
Now loosened, releasing me to breathe
anew, To rediscover the melody of my
own voice.
I unfurl my wings, stretching towards
the sun, Each feather a testament to
resilience, Each beat a defiance against
your manipulation.
I blossom, not in spite of you, but
because of you, For in your absence, I
find the space to grow, To bloom into
the radiant being I was meant to be.
No longer defined by your gaslighting
whispers, I embrace the jagged edges
of my authenticity, Each scar a badge
of honor, each flaw a masterpiece.

"Healing is not about forgetting the past, but about embracing the lessons it taught us, and looking forward to the brighter future it paved the way for."

In the mirror's reflection, I see her glow, A woman of grace, with a spirit that flows. Through trials and triumphs, she's grown and evolved, In her own skin, she's beautifully resolved.
With each passing day, she blooms anew, Embracing her flaws, and her strengths too. For in loving herself, she's found the key, To cherish the woman she's come to be.

Today I'm letting go of your toxic
hold,
I reclaim my power, fierce and bold.
No longer tethered to your twisted
game,
I rise from ashes, shedding off the
shame.
With each step forward, I leave
behind The chains of manipulation,
unkind.
So take your new supply, I set you
free, For in your absence, I find
clarity.
I heal, I thrive, I reclaim my worth,
No longer captive to your toxic mirth.

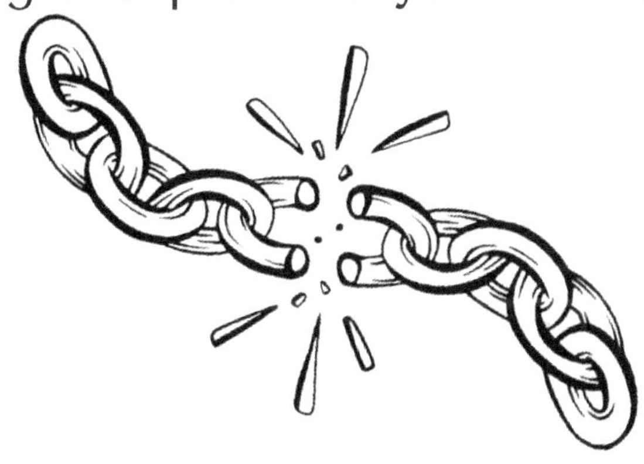

In Beauty's eyes, the Beast beheld,
A soul untouched, a heart
compelled.
Through trials faced and truths
unveiled,
Their bond grew strong, their love
Fulfilled.
For in each soul, a beauty lies,
Beyond the surface, where love
defies.
In scars and flaws, we find our
grace,
A mirror of the human race.
So let us learn from Beauty's tale,
To see beyond the surface veil.
For in embracing both beauty and
beast,
We find the essence of love,
released.

-Beauty And The Beast

Closing a chapter in life bears a striking resemblance to a curtain call in a grand performance. Just as the curtain descends at the end of a play, signaling the conclusion of one act and the beginning of another, so too does closing a chapter mark the end of a significant period and the commencement of something new.

My final Reflection

Moving on doesn't mean forgetting or dismissing the past; rather, it's about integrating those experiences into our narrative, weaving them into the fabric of our being. It's about honoring the journey, the struggles, and the triumphs, and allowing them to shape us into wiser, more compassionate individuals.

As we move forward, we carry with us the invaluable lessons learned – the importance of self-love, the power of resilience, and the beauty of forgiveness. These lessons become our compass, guiding us toward a future filled with promise and possibility. And in embracing both the scars and the wisdom gained along the way, we embark on a journey of healing, growth, and transformation.

Author Thoughts

Writing poetry is like... awakening a part of your soul that has been slept on. No one knew you would bring so much impact and passion by just expressing your words in the form of freestyle, bars and lines. I grew up in a structured up bringing I am the fourth child born to my amazing parents. I enjoyed reading and writing growing up, if I had a thought I would write it down, I always kept a notebook on me or around me and would enjoy making to do lists to keep me on task of what the day may bring. I developed a interest to poetry my 12th grade year in English class. I really admired Maya Angelo and William Shakespeare. My first poem was horrible I'm not going to lie, it was about a crush I never got a chance to even speak too. I wrote more and more until I filled up a book with 100 poems from my childhood sadly I can't find these but if I do I would make a book with them as a reminder of how far I have came in writing poems and stories. My name is Victoria Richardson and I am a poet.

Letter From The Author

To my dear readers, I wrote this book with the intention of it serving as the beginning of something important to me and, perhaps, to all of you. In this chapter of my narrative, I wanted you to experience the intersection of love, loss, passion, and beauty. Since life isn't all sunshine and butterflies, I called my book The Butterfly Effect because, although life is full of ups and downs, it can also be both chaotic and beautiful.

Please feel free to express yourself on
the next few pages.

notes

notes

notes

notes

notes

notes

notes

notes

notes

notes

notes

notes

notes

notes